# chameleon

published by

MANNAMEAD

P · R · E · S · S

october 1986
to
january 1988

starring

# terrence neal haley

guest appearances

by

**simon smith**

**brian else**

&

a cameo

by

**lyne osbourne-turner**

a measure of this script
is dedicated to stuart
who was a good friend to me
when i first hit plymouth

he was like an old tweed jacket
coming apart at the seams
but still with a good few years wear left


*steering wheel ears*
*chasing flames*
*burning ends meet at middle*


seem to be cast
upon the vagaries of fate
yet again


*settlin in plymouth*
*checkin the city*
*for life-style an love*

*am leading a charmed life*
*but i dont know what for*


one can conceive an idea
and execute it
but it doesnt mean
one really *believes* in that idea
it's just a thought among many
some get realised
some dont
it doesnt matter


must realise
i'm writing for two media
my journal
and books


**i am the wet paint**
**to peoples understanding**

*present*

dont want to die in obscurity

*future*

will not die in obscurity

*past*

did not die in obscurity

scene one
take two
*haiku here i come*

*caterwauling cats*
*wind shakes frame*
*crash lid*

*to capture nature in towns*
*where it shouldnt be*
*thats haiku*

dont want to be
   caught up in words
but the moment
   but will the words be caught?

*terry reached for a drink*
*dragonfly a pen*
*both dipped*

*we drink*
*& toast each other*
*terry & fly*

*we're still squeezing*
*the spots off society*
*and civilisation*

dont seem to be mixing
with famous faces
so will have to mix with
famous places

*if my baby dont come*
*for herself to me*
*will relieve myself*
*of her key*

*flowers purple*
*to the wall cling*
*pseudo spring*


spent my whole life hangin aroun
spent my whole life lisnin to
other people sounoff
which i dont get offon
which is rather off-not-on


spent too much money
with little return
return to sender
no plagiarism intended


it's my ken
not kith or kin

would be a sin


*the longer you live*
*the longer you die*
*the longer you sing*
*the longer you cry*

rain
wake
rain
drink
rain
sleep
rain
wake
rain
drink
rain
sleep
rain

another day
wiped away


too long
i've played truant
from life


too long
i couldnt cope
with strife


but now
i'm starting up
and how !


**the one thing
i envy about women
is that
they dont make a mess
when they masturbate**

crystal frontiers bar the way
from here to there
a line divides my wanderings
always looking out
from in instead
of in from out


*s t r a i n i n g the strings
of friendship
somehow s e v e r i n g*


can't be a nondescript
in the factories
havent found my métier yet
but still plod on

### by simon

Cast and setting for :-

*The Ballad of Glencoe*
*(A Tale of Provincial Doings)*

Brian was a big bad biker
Real cool in a banana top
Terry the pugnacious poet
Adventurer to the last
And myself; laconic, loquacious, lethargic?
Cove

Glencoe. The centre of the known
Universe, Mecca for masters and students
Of philosophy, advisor to government
                           everywhere
Casserole of culinary expertise,
                           lexicographers
And warriors of ancient lineage,
                           purveyors of
Quality teas since 1865
Take it as read then, that throughout
These wee doggerels, Glencoe is the
                           blazing sun
That brings heat and light into the
                           vacuum of
The firmament.

                        *(Classics follow...)*

*by brian*

Glencoe
Three it is instead of five
Who dwell the 'coe
And make their lives
Doing dole
Means there's time
For Contemplate
    Agitate
    Deliberate
To make the rhythm
Rhyme.

*by me*

ode to 'glencoe'

laconic lolled
oblivious whatever
analytical what?

**both by brian**

I'm one and a half
I am
And no one understands
Everything of interest
Is taken from my hands

I mean what's wrong
With scissors
What's wrong with matches too?
I'm only playing with them
To see what they can do?

*Live life*
*As life*
*For life*

### by simon

The time is ripe
To smoke a pipe
And tell a tale
Of mice and men
In days of old
Roamed warriors bold
What happened then?

I know
They fought for kings
And met in rings
Brave and just
They battled for right
With spear and sword
All covered in gore
Give us a light.


### for simon

stick with me kid
and you'll go nowhere

got a black belt
in paranoia
but only 3rd dan

## by brian

Conform
Conform
From the day you are born
It's not that you're wrong
Only different


## simon's answer

Confirm
Confirm
That you're willing to learn
It's not that you're dull
Only different

Imitate
Imitate
Until it's too late
And then you might see
You're not all that great.

the swinging 60's
the austere 70's
the haunted 80's


**Q.** what occupation would you really
like given a completely free choice?
**A.** plymouth – south seas
ahoy!


never set foot
on the white doorstep
of england agen


only dabbled in life
never taken it seriously
or it me

*by simon*

Hot chestnut
Charring
Pop

*by me*

hot chestnut
roasting
pop

*the fact that the chestnut is roasting*
*makes the word 'hot' superfluous*

chestnut
roasting
pop !

### *2 by Brian*

What would you do
If dreams came true
To find you're dreaming still?

It's funny how we stay the same
Our lives remaining pretty plain
Sometimes a laugh, sometimes a cry
Sometimes a truth, sometimes a lie
However, as our life goes on
It's usually to the same old song
Then at once you're all about
A wave comes in to oust you out
You're cast upon the sea of life
You drown two times
And reborn thrice
Hang on and ride the storm
It is for this that you were born
Excitement courses through your veins
To out-sail doubts and bail out pains
Until a calm returns once more
With you washed upon your *sure*.

times were gettin hard
pickin coal form the yard
the days were gettin bleak
then the snows began


hobnailed boots clinked on
                    cobbles
the boys in blue gave us
                    troubles
the nights were freezin
when the snows began


*so fight with your might*
*agenst the Right*
*fight with whats left*
*for the Left*


half a pound of butter for
            all our needs
but before i could utter
"eggs milk an cheese"
was kicked outta the door
            into the storm


theres mountains for all
an lakes by the score
but doled out with dollops
an teeny weeny drops

*so fight with your might*
*agenst the Right*
*fight with whats left*
*for the Left*


"been down so long
it looks like up" someone sed
"kept down so long
will i ever get up?" i've jus sed


got so little it makes me a
                        thief
nowt cumin in so moonlightjn an
                        stealin
steal from the streets steal
        from the shops
jus one jump ahead of the cops


*so fight with your might*
*agenst the Right*
*fight with whats left*
*for the Left*


fight tooth an claw
agenst their law
with head hands an feet
out on the streets

### simons lament

hovering on the verge of happiness
waiting for depression to come a-knocking
will the door be open
will the will be broken?


magpie on the maypole
collecting children all around
pipers paid whistle em away


*life at the moment*
*is the lowest common denominator*


**love life – nil**
**fuck life – minimal**
**so dont bother about**
**no action replay**

*tearing myself away*
*yet again*
*from another family?*

**Soulcialists of the World unite**
**youve got nothing to lose**
**but the Right**

do women have the power over men
because of their sex
because men want it
is this a fallacy?

dont women walk home alone
thinking about a cock between their legs
as men think of putting it there?

are men the weaker sex
because they want it more
do women corner the market in it?

towards a new dawn
towards a new beginning
towards a new dawn
onward to optimism


push back the darkness
push back the veil
push back the darkness
go forward youll not fail


let the light shine forth
let the rays be cast around
let the light shine forth
dispel the fears and doubts


here comes a new awareness
here comes a new ideal
here comes a new awareness
pick up pieces of your dream

*next three by brian*

Everything he didn't want
Is all that keeps him going

The seed he didn't want to grow
Are now the ones he's sowing.

*A seed kept in a packet*
*Is how I see my life*
*Searching for a sowing ground*
*After being planted so many times*
*before*
*These roots are tired of retracting*
*They've searched for nourishment*
*time and time again*
*Sandy barren soil is all this seed*
*has got*
*Fertile ground has been there,*
*conditions have not.*

Reality sets in
Cutting a deep and open wound
Across your life
Exposing you before your dreams and
ideals

What was
And what could have been
Are miles apart, now distant echoes
Ringing confusion in your head

Round and round you go
Until a dizzy stubbornness
Sets your course
Reality sets in
Bringing you back to life.

**by me**

life is just around the corner
but how many corners have i turned?
life is just around the corner
i'm down a dead-end street and it's
no return

Romanticisms being
bludgeoned by Realism
but i won't go under


life is a lost
bunch of keys
that you dont expect to find
but is a bonus
if you do


*o.k.j.c.*
*"tomorrow will take care of itself"*
*but will it worry about me?*

weakly limping
with millions on dole
week by week / cheek by jowl


shall i shan't i
bright then dull
hang the washing up to dry


clambering up this ladder of life
slipping down the slithery snake
back to the beginning


crap rap stuff
the sounds of now?
if so doe wanna  know

*God was elsewhere when i phoned Him*
                    *up today*
*i called His special number*
*but a recorded voice answered*
*"He's away on holiday"*


*"He's never there when needed"*
*said after the bleeps had faded*
*"so next time He's in His office*
*can you get Him to call me back?*


*you see i've got this problem*
*minute to all the rest*
*my girl has upped and left me*
*spread her wings and flew the nest*


*He knows i love her dearly*
*broke my heart when she said*
                    *'goodbye'..."*


*just then an extension was lifted*
*and a voice said "this is God"*
*"hallelujah" my exclamation*
*but then my coins ran out...*

remember me baby?
i'm the one you always said you
                              loved
    remember me baby?
why then did you say goodbye?


    remember me sweetheart?
i'm the one whose heart you broke
    remember me sweetheart?
tore our lives apart at one foul
                              stroke


are you happy with your lover
how many other lovers by the wayside
left upside down turned all around
    when you said goodbye?


    been paid back over odds
    but got lost along the way
    emotions count the cost
    and left with the bill to pay


    of the hurt and of the pain
    an echoing empty house
    the cheating and the lies
    am sick of this same refrain...

*even a bird*
*chortles Haiku from the beginning*
*but we must learn*


*peg east? peg west?*
*dont know whats best*
*which way the wind blows*


*fluttering pennants twirling feather*
*drone of bagpipes*
*Sutton Marina*

*J.C. was a little late today*
*the World had blown itself away*
*the appointment He had made*
*was made for a later date*

*His diary read the year 2000*
*the New Millennium He was bound*
*for here on Earth, but when He*
                              *arrived*
*it could not be found*

*He swore, taking His own name*
                    *in vain*
*"Oh Lord" an oath proclaimed*
*"I'd promised to return*

*Big G will not be happy*
*when He hears the news*
*He's probably heard already*
*so it's about time I blew*

*how I wished I'd read the Bible*
*then I'd know just what to do*
*but I was too busy living it*
*not with the Old mind you but*
                        *the New*

*My whole Life and Death (I may*
*add) leading up to this*
*all those reservations waiting*
*to be filled*
*looks like I'm along with the*
*other 3 million*
*joining the ol' dole queue"*

### by simon

The fields of knowledge: Sown with
Only the finest seed, fed with
Pure organic fertilisers, and reaped
With utmost delicacy.

**(Book? What fucking book?)**

women *aerate*
men *flatulate*
horses **fart**


                    the vultures and jackals
                   turned up as per usual
                to fight amongst the scraps



every night an alcoholic haze
every morn awake to a new day
if you lose a penny youll certainly
        lose a pound
for whichever way you choose youll
        still be found
the tentacles of past reach out

### by brian

Late for a date with old J.C.
To save the world was His mission to be
When He got here we were all gone
So He twiddled His thumbs and thought of
                                   a song

He wandered around and looked at the mess
And while He was looking He found
                    something blessed
A book it was
The Bible its name
And while He was reading the New bit
He read of His fame

"I didn't know that I meant so much
To so many people so out of touch
Such a shame I'm too late to save them
                    from sin
I suppose they just didn't know where to
                    begin

Well I suppose I can fix it up with me
                    Dad
To give them a chance of which they'll
                    be glad
I suppose some deserve it for trying so
                    hard
Dad'll see I was late from me clocking-in
                    card"

i stopped stared then saw her
   in the arms of another
stopped stared then saw her
   kissing my best friend


i stopped started forward but turned
                      away
   i could not confront them
stopped started forward but turned
                      away
   wishing i had no friend


   a friend that saved my life
   a friend that stole my wife
a buddy thru thick and thru thin
   please anybody but him


does he touch her like i used to do
   in places i cannot tell
does she kiss him and whisper sweet
                      words?
   oh god i think i'm in hell

a hell right here on this earth
when heaven was once by her side
purgatory's dealt me these cards
with the ace up its sleeve who's my
                                    bride


what do i say when i'm home
or drinking with my buddy alone
to the one that gave me her heart
and a friend that tore us apart?


*also j.c.*
*it's not tomorrow i'm worried about*
*but today*

nuclear pistols in their hands
to wipe out all our lands
the eagle and the bear
with claw and paw
clutching crushing

the World asunder
for all to own

                         kicked by u.k.
                knocked down under foot
                   trampled in channel
              "you won't smother me"
                         . i shout!

theres nothing to fear but fear itself
nothing to believe but belief itself

if the slugs on the thorn
and the grasshoppers a burden
then the turtle has gone from this land


holding myself for ransom
i threaten the world
listen to me or else


dont just want to wander
the highways and byways of town
but of this planet

its not so much
i wanna be on the gravy-train
just wouldnt mind a bit of dripping


*wind whispers to eyes*
*"we belong"*
*ears see rain say*
*"be strong"*


killing time
fill in time
my life at present

i love the actual physical act
of writing so much
that i take an ineffable delight
in making out a shopping list

*my poems*
*are my progeny*
*my line through time*

triptych poems
tripping upstairs
let slip

another night alone
another night on my own
another night of loneliness
another
       and
            another...


if i didnt have my writing
i think i'd be deranged
i fancy its the only thing
that keeps me going


sane whose sane?


reckon i'm going insane
the 'in' gets in the way
no matter what you say
onward i struggle


to struggle to live
to live to fight
to fight to win
to win to achieve


achievement in death
death fruits life
regenerations progress
repeating ••• — — ••• ••• — — ••• ••• — — ••• •

its times like this i wished i'd
                  listened
listened to what my ol' mama sed
"what did she say?" i hear you
                       question
dont know cos i never listened


its times like this i wished i'd
                    heeded
heeded my ol' papas advice
"what was that?" i hear you ask me
dont know cos i never heeded


all the times thru my life people
                  have told me
told me just what to do
but i still end up in situations
                      with
'but i just dont understand' blues


in my matrix is the answer and the
                 answer is '42'
dont know about the answer
but what about the question?
cos ive got 'the hitch-hikers
           guide to the galaxy' blues

'life universe and everything?'
all those questions and i dont
               know what to do
but all i want is 'a nice cup of
                    tea'
cos ive got 'the hitch-hikers
      guide to the galaxy' blues

*you are what you believe*
*nobody else might*
*but does it matter?*

following a dream
  but i dont know
    what it is

walk proud & tall
listen to the call
the call thats in us all

listen to the beat
the beat thats in your feet
then take it to the street

listen to the sounds
the sounds are all around
listen theyll be found

in the wind & in the rain
youll hear the same refrain
youll hear the music played

the music of the spheres
listen with your ears
listen with your heart

theres music everywhere
everywhere is there
listen and somehow

open ears the sound
open eyes around
listen your song belongs

*anyhow j.c.*
*not today*
*but now*

dont lose your dreams
dont lose your visions
elect and select
for your dreams & for
your morrows

what day is it tomorrow?
i dont know
but whatever it is i'll find it

everybody sez
that i remind them
of somebody else
but i dont even
remind me of me


*poetry*
*to distil thoughts*
*to words*


its not the thought thats exciting
but the elation to the thought
for when reflecting on that thought
it hasnt got the excitement
cos theres no elation

you moan when you dont write
and moan when you do
you criticise all bloody time
the same old beat back-biting street
the same old noses around curtains
calling
and kippers smell would last a week


i'm a surbibor
i'm ere to stay
a surbibor
abe cum all this way

i'm still ere
still shoutin out
loud and clear
still wanna know
whatsit all about?

doe wanna know
yor ways & means
yoube fucked it up
webe eard the screams

berate yourself the marquee falls
piano pounding out
candles flicker pin-pointing souls
to sin agen in gardens fair

betook himself to garrets bare
the haunted winds swept austere
a paradise compared to now


*one persons idealism*
*is anothers realism*


chemical trees
forest streets
u/s of a

got the pedestrian blues
pedestrian blues wearing out my shoes
machine drums the fact
an officer reiterates he's a nasty man


bass-line bothers the bobbys beat
he's still on his feet
rhythms reach discordants rash
fast-food flicks across his mouth
and forests cover every street


ale swills & bellys bulge
fought from my fathers forge
this counterfeit life


"we all indulge" has been said
'thoughts are swords'
menu reads 'egg chips & beans'
junk manifests itself


waitress screams reuben reels
weve made a mess of everything

jamie jams cathy spells
terry tries as quintet fails
rich scatter brains
as blue suede shoes


her name cannot recall
face from a crowd
advertising fame
confused the issue


a glance at back
confirms the fact
that scratches count the score

searched amongst the shadows
for spaces in between
umbras tell a story
when not knowing whats in
                              store

cast amongst the legions
their numbers foretell doom
symbols of religion
of not knowing where you are

cannot tell the difference
three wise men knew the score
gifts they brought triumphant
civilisations cradled nought

from the deep equatorial jungles of
africa
to the wide open plains of america
my mind soars
but my presence stays
in this room in this house in plymouth


sunlight soap and hope
have kept me young
en-route to 46


prowling the strip
in my cool blue dudes
since i heard the news

staggering towards eighty-eight
in more ways than one
one thin man


fuelled by fame
pursue my name
chase the elusive high

head for goal
sell my soul?
these are reasons why

the answer lies before me
but blinded by conceit
opaqueness hides the question
clumsy continued beat

*j.c.*
*now*
*here*

walked over Faeces Fields
down around Pervert Park
strolled up The Plain
for a drink in 'The Grave'

the voice of blood sings through my veins
past generations echo round my brain
but can only catch a line or two
can only hear the odd song
here and there

the acrid smell of a fresh lit match
assailed my nostrils, i stopped suddenly
trying to control my breathing, shocked
that i hadnt heard the scratch of match
    i edged forward cautiously and
nervously, trying to marshal all my
limited fighting skills, of what i'd
actually done and read, mainly read
    thanking the gods that i was wearing
a decent pair of practical shoes, i felt
a little reassured, knowing i could
always run if my fantasy bruce lee
surprise attack failed
    i wondered if i shouldnt run there
and then? or should i say, sidle away
cockroach-like...

root-less people
in a haunted land
austerity passed them by
and a wilderness they found

*I am the One who died for you*
       *entangled My life for you*
*carried the cross was no need to*
*cried out in pain called My Fathers name*
       *but did He come through?*


*slipped salvation but had no need to*
*skipped across the seas but did you*
                             *believe?*
       *stopped wind and rain*
       *but could I stop the pain?*


*a crown of thorns kings cloak stripped*
                             *from My back*
*you washed your hands no turning back*
*your fault or Mine? it was written*
*but still you laughed as I was stricken*


*you strung Me up children all cried "no"*
       *did you listen? you never do*
       *they have the answer*
       *but can I blame you?*
*all are blinded by whats gone before*


       *you all could not face it*
       *except a chosen few*
       *put My life before Me*
       *the point is will you?*

this person stands before you
stripped of all illusions
a quivering mass of nothingness
tender to the touch


i tee for green
taking rough with smooth
mainly rough


the sands of time
running fast
and reaper calls the tune


splurt it out barked major hal
minors react with like
its not such a bad idea
to go agenst beliefs

cynicism sits beneath the ego
is it love or just a figure?
gnawing doubts eat into confidence


                    i am beacon into eighty-eight
          enlightening the future from the past
                    forward i stride through time


living on borrowed time
strung out at the end of line
pushing the limit to its most
running for the finishing post

always out of reach
never seem to make the meet
rushing for the rainbows end
pot of gold never my friend

### by lynne osbourne-turner

Do you know that God above
Created you for me to love
He picked you out from all the rest
Because He knew I loved you best
I had a heart and it was true
But now it's gone from me to you
Take care of it darling as I have done
For you have two and I have none.

*re. j.c.*
*throughout book*
*recurring theme*
*piece of music*


*no chronology*
*as in 'report'*
*orchestrate a symphony*

tidy up the world i cannot
perfect beings do we want?
j.c. short with disciples
bit of a know-all if you ask


pretentious & smart-assed people i
                          cannot stand
              guts swill
keep your mind together else infiltrate


always cared it kept me going
frightened to leave himself with anybody
still serving apprenticeship
running blue-coat trailing


belted at back no turning back
internal enquiry only answer
that keeps the lid on
to the mould beneath


but keep on nagging
belay the new state
that cause dissension
this is my home-land
its all inside me
there must be give & take

expect nobody i aint the one
he could not give the good or take
did not believe he would not know
took himself beside the tow


that barge on hands & feet
stalactites they drip on down
would not believe it is no worth
when catching shells inside themselves


    /     /     /   /     /   /
    /     /     /   /     /   /
    /     /     /   /     /   /
    /     /     /   /     /   /  /  /


    /     /     /   /     /   /  /
    /     /     /   /     /   /  /
    /     /     /   /     /   /  /
    /     /     /   /     /   /  /

no rule in life so dont get excited
all those bridges crossed over many
                           waters
        cliff face confronts
insurmountable barriers i can jump


furrowed fields come into view
yellow leaves swirl surrounding
smoke trails from fingertips
mingle in clouds midst pools


socrates died tidily
but you & me know better


                    *look beneath the labels*
                     *titles sometimes hide*
                    *from cradle to grave*
                *keep wonderment in mind*

### by brian

The marrow moon harvest
Reaps a mellow mind
From hungers satisfaction

Then the trio trudged
Through Turdy Turf
To total their thirst

Homeward bound
Three friends are found

Six spliffing lima trippers
Sensing storm
Heads homewards bound
Over Sound
Observe autumnal aura.

your perfume upon my pillow
your scent upon the sheets
remembrance of things past
till again we meet


marvel at this moment
postmortems i cannot cope
rememberings the only hope
when you have gone


grab the glitter silver-red
shed dreams for real
catch the meaning in this song
you know where it belongs


finger tips they tell the story
lightly on each others skin
exhausted until daybreak
      then again begin

yor name is on this bullet
cos i'm pointin this loaded gun
i sed yor name is on this bullet
cos i'm pointin this loaded gun
so lower yor defences
cos i'm cummin right on in


got my finger on the trigger
& i'm squeezin it right now
i sed i've got my finger on the trigger
& i'm squeezin it right now
cos i can feel ya quiver
i'm gonna shoot ya up & how


get down on your knees mah baby
open your mouth & pray
i sed get down on yor knees mah baby
open yor mouth & pray
cos mah weapon is a-gunnin
& yor gonna catch the spray


look out baby i'm re-loadin
gettin ready to shoot again
i sed look out baby i'm re-loadin
gettin ready to shoot again
this time theres no resistance
yor lookin forward to the same

bonkin is for beginners
its love that counts
if you cannot catch the trimmins
lust labours lost


"dont just wet your willie"
sed the joker to the crown
emperor played his cards right
nine-hundred concubines


dont serve up all the answers
to questions that were unreal
after the initial explosions
lie back & youll feel


*keeping my poetic hand in*
*i carve a poem that reeks*
*of trying not lying to myself*
*i know its worth*

constant sordid dramas in this sink of
        life i do not need
scattered sentiments abound the floor
        of time i do not want
house-proud relationships the answer
to a question of untidy emotions
spick & span feelings not what i ask
confrontations at cross-purposes
        become the norm
alcohol accusations i will not face
cannot touch those tacky units
        and floor strewn agitations
        layers of dirty linen
as i stagger through that door

cannot be like these folks
achilles he cuts my tendon
quasimodo humps complaint
quartet quivers in anticipation
this hidden book thought near
                    completion


hone my talons never knew i had
she taught me knowledge would i take?
face to face flashed on my brain
but i knew she would not look below
the mills & boon trite titles


miasma labels lie in wait
to those that cannot tell
the difference is only in between
facts chosen to what you believe
youre still waiting at the gate


you sub-titled your emotions
bold statements could hardly reveal
the feeling of reality
that lies beneath the skin
of what you think is going on

"blurt it out" you hear me shout
dive deep in words dont hide the fact
of what you & me try to talk about
let you & me try another tack
but you dont want to hear


i honed my talons you sharpened claws
but was the game for real?
lived life in labels never looked
                    beneath
all that time hidden behind doors
and drowned in your own crocodile
                    tears


cuffed my wrists i would not button up
out in open but youre still in a tent
campers scream they would not believe
put out the candle when shedding
                    clothes
youre conscious but still in a dream

speed-freaks down d.f. streets
docile fools keep on snorting more
weak-willed non-contenders
friday girls think they know the score


grab the cash from yankees hands
buck blacks stash swop hash for weed
reds under bed when making plans
home-growers plant the seed


sailors raped girls sneer with glee
matlows homeward bound
a.i.d.s each other with a payment
extract the highest fee


*to become involved*
*is pain*
*to not become involved*
*is also pain*
*the path to salvation*
*seems fraught with pain*
*can one escape?*

melancholia beguiles this autumn
                              eve
sadness surrounds as bonfire burns
tongues of flame entangle night
yearnings that can never be


tears flood my face
obliterate the trace of a smile up
                         front
forced for friends and foes alike
vanish into night


mists meet at corners
moon shines down disjointed
years that swirl are trod beneath
scattered memories an untidy heap


sighs escape sobs still shake
an almost empty shell
wander wearily no place to rest
recall that care-worn face

*dedicated to mother*

i knew it was time tafall
cos i'd got nuthin talose
from that one girl down the hall
got me the bed-sit syndrum blues


i knew that as i fell
that i waz gonna lose
an could easily tell
you bout the bed-sit syndrum blues


bare bulb burnin down threadbare stairs
wallpaper of a darkened hue
corridor echoed taother lives ensnared
in the bed-sit syndrum blues


softly knockin then harder still
kids screams abound as animals in a zoo
knowin i'd afta swallow lifes bitter
                              pill
of the bed-sit syndrum blues


door opens boiled cabbage smells
                    outward spills
battlin with cheap perfume an my cue
baby-bellins over-cooked food fills
the room of the bed-sit syndrum blues

she answers tadistraction then sez
                    "cum right on in"
each seat is filled with week-old news
its what i call livin in sin
in the bed-sit syndrum blues


2nd she's got no coffee & 3rd she's got
                    no tea
afta 1st "do i wanna drink" 4 got no
                    booze
5thly wondered "whats happenin ta me?"
in this bed-sit syndrum blues


standin there with nuthin in my hand
                    cept my own cigarette
"ave i finally succumbed to these
                    depths?" i mused
still standin there half-listenin thinking
                    "no not yet"
in this bed-sit syndrum blues


mumbled half-hearted "bout goin to the
                    bar"
sure glad when she refused
gratefully closed the door an thanked my
                    lucky stars
still fightin them bed-sit syndrum blues

i remember it well knockin on her front
                                    door
she sed "justep on in an take a seat"
straight way handed me a drink from a
                            pack of four
"woman afta my own heart" thought i
                "what a nice way to meet"
sed "would ya like a drink this friday?"
                        an she sed "sure"
since then i've bin goin back for more


friday came roun slowly waitin was such
                            a bore
"cum right in an take a chair" she
                called "an grab a drink
i'll ave me another & roll a splif cos
                        i've juscored
fancy droppin some d.f.'s?" she asked
                which made me think
"okay" sed i "shall we hit the pubs?"
                    an she sed "sure"
an so i've bin goin back for more

well we ended up at her place an finished
                          on the floor
from more ways than one i tell ya but
                          only so much
leave it tayor imagination but say that
          at each others clothes we tore
then from floor tabedroom we helped
                          each other up
"shall we do that again?" i asked an she
                          sed "sure"
an so i've bin goin back for more


i went on back taher place with
                  ya-know-what tathe fore
she again received me sayin "cum right on
                          in"
from scratches on back ya could count the
                          score
i lost the race but wasnt out tawin
"would ya like an action replay?" an she
                          sed "sure"
cos ya know i've bin goin back for more

bin back now a few times an every time
theres more
booze bing pills an all that lust
but a little voice inside me still
questions the allure
an i keep on goin back there as ya know
i must
cos when i say "shall we do it agen?"
an she sez "sure"
ya know i'll keep goin back for
more



progressive pain that washes over me
as the day wears on
each move i make an effort
each turn of the body an ache
hurts more than i realised
deaden with d.f.'s & booze
head for home & brave face
an up front attitude to hide the trace
of pain that racks my frame

volcano in the distance has given up
                              its ghost
but i espy with my little eye a tiny
                     trickle of smoke
razor blade smile an Chatterton drink
poisons my mind so i dunno wot to
                                   think


Barbican Belle was her name
she introduced me to Mary Jane
foun myself in bed with them both
but when i looked roun Jane had
            vanished in a haze of smoke


the tailor he demanded that he would
                           cut my suit
the builder he commanded units to be
                                  built
bullets kept on flyin i could not take
                         the flack
u no wot i did my friends? i jushit
                   them tracks

stood relieved in Princetown beside
                    the prison walls
arguein contentedly i did not hear him
                              call
missed out all together when the
                         warder shouted out
"roll up for illusions" as i walked
                            across the moat


entered an open court-yard portcullis
                         dropped with a clang
turned to run but i waz trapped by fans
justhen Belle appeared beckonin me aside
"take a toke on this" she sed "then
                              maybe we'll hide"


she pushed me up a passage an opened
                    out a door
"go right in" she shoved i foun it
                    had no floor
ended in a dungeon laughter all aroun
but i waznt even smilin cos i'd jusrun
                              agroun

water then started seepin in issuein
                    from every crak
Moses not my cell-mate he could not
                    hold it bak
i floated to the window so i thought to
                    take a look
Barnacle Bill rowed on by seated on
                    this book

in his hand waz Mary Jane an a smile
                              upon his face
he heard my pleas gave me the keys an
                    sed "get bak in the race"
Tu Fu waz out fishin an so he cast a
                              line
reeled me in stashed his takle an sed
                    "we're justin time"

D.H. came by with my mate Walt we lined
          up for the start
Li Po he stood there laughin the pistol
          at my heart
"youve got a long way to go my friend
                    an it can enright here"
but aroun the battlements strolled Bashō
          who called out "have no fear"

stood in bamboo gardens drinkin our
       rice wine
champagne waz also bubblin we waz
       doin fine
then Belle made her appearance the band
            began to play
friends joined in the chorus as i took
         her hand they all sang
           "get the hell away!"


*cast off my illusions*
*i stand before you*
*as i am*


preaching Socialism without
would i preach it with?

Johnny Business he had none in that part
           of town
wrong side of tracks no turning back
when he met Irene Innocent at the
              high-school prom

       he asked her for a dance
she thought "shall i take a chance?"
her friends looked on in amazement
but deep down they all wished that theyd
            been asked

Irenes night went in a dream
Johnny never held a girl like that
"a drive-in movie?" a question he pressed
her head said "no" but her heart answered
              "yes"

their drive-in date went by so fast a
         movie unremembered
   each held hands gazed deep in eyes
Irene waited for the move Johnny would
        not make
cos he was hand & tongue-tied for the
        first time in his life

and so the meetings carried on
spiral-bound their lives entwined
looked on in horror by families both
"stook up" his folks would cry
hers clamoured "he's a bad boy"

their dates grew much more frequent
they fell full deeper in love
parents could not believe understand
and so condemned it
so announcing their engagement they fled
to the anger of all concerned

stood centre stage the crowd looked on
orchestra played to rise of baton
chorus in wings voices raised singing
scenery made by Johnny painted by Irenes
hand

audience in anticipation were startled
at first lines
attentively listened then warmed to
appreciation as action started to
unfold
their spoken words danced round the
stage
echoed for all to hear

the patrons sat enraptured could not
believe their ears
lives played out agenst all odds
but each character knew the score
condemnation now no more as the curtain
dropped

*re.queues*

*the shortest is the slowest*
*and the quickest is the long*

my life began in violence
    both from my mom & dad
them backstreets were my
                    battlefields
    it was the only fun i had
a chip was on each shoulder
    as well as in my bag
i beat down all who disagreed
    cos youll know me
fight force with force
    is my philosophy


i fought at home i fought at
                    school
    i fought to have my say
i fought my friends & enemies
    i fought both night & day
i fought the crooks & cops alike
    cos they got in the way
for when you get down to brass
                    tacks
    then you will agree
that my way of life is the only
                  way to be

you talk of 'love' i talk of 'hate'
    that difference will separate
cos you believe its everlasting
    and think its just a spate
that i'll get over but i bet you mate
    that the facts when they confront
               you
then you will see
    that youre frightened of situations
i'm not you see


all my life i've been fighting
    fighting till the day i die
but your lives have been buffeted by
               fate
    you never even try
i won't even make a comment
    its not worth it i'll just sigh
youll always never be nothing youll
               just be
but me i'll go out fighting
            fighting to be free

i went back to Baltimore
   i travelled there last fall
met my ol' mate Gentleman Jim
   a friend you do recall
the leaves they were a-blazing
   lay thickly on the ground
autumn sky was hazy
   but you could not be found


i met Big Jim in a bar
   drinking whisky & some beer
i asked him if he'd seen you
   he replied "no not here"
went out into the night
   dejected & upset
met Molly on the corner
   who said "let you & me forget"


forgot what i was there for
   was weary with defeat
but then could not be bothered
   when Molly turned on the heat
my clothes were shed
   my conscience fled
when in her bed
   with Molly between the sheets

went out into the morning
    around about mid-day
fell in a bar asked for a jar
    but before i could pay
Big Jim was in his pocket
    & then he ordered more
"no my friend  you should not"
    he replied "okay i know the score"


Torpedo Pete & Pseudo Sim
    both of them rolled in
the gang appeared
    drinks disappeared
paid by Gentleman Jim
    drinks flashed around
still stood my ground
    but i knew i could not win


i crawled out in the night
    & bumped into some feet
i clawed up clothes to view its face
    to see who i would meet
the voice awakened memories
    of days long past & gone
melodious speech of Actor Jon
    a sound i can't repeat

the words he said as spoken
    were "welcome back in town
i'll help you up lets drink a cup
    i see youve run aground"
so down the street we reeled
    singing songs of old
burst in a joint they saw our point
    & ordered all around

the room began a-spinning
    i was feeling ill
"have another drink my friend"
    but i had had my fill
just then my head exploded
    lay splattered on the floor
so i picked up all the pieces
    & headed for the door

i fell onto the sidewalk
    where i lay & could not move
scattered thoughts assembled
    what was i trying to prove
that i could live without you?
    but i knew it wasnt true
so i headed back to Blighty
    & the bed-sit syndrum blues

i landed at the airport
    & stumbled customs-bound
they searched my bags & person
    & a broken heart was found
i staggered to a taxi
    but before i could fall in
you appeared before me
    & said "lets try agen"

Jim held a reception
    invited all our friends
Molly poured out all the drinks
    & toasted to made amends
Pete & Pseudo both drank up
    then began to weep
Jon made a speech i can't repeat
    cos we all fell slow asleep

*i was born & belong to this planet*
*so i should be allowed*
*basically to go wherever i like*

Trivial Pursuits was the game
    a game i could not pursue
but i'm quite good at pursuing
    cos i'm pursuing you

Ludo was a lead in
    you said "okay lets play"
but you set up a road-block
    your head got in the way

then we played Backgammon
    but i could not keep track
cos i'm not Lucky Lucan
    you told me to back-track

Snakes & Ladders next we tried
    i thought i had a chance
but all you did was climb away
    and not slide down on romance

i thought we'd try Monopoly
    but you would not come through
i set up house you bought me out
    when i tried monopolising you

from there we went to Cluedo
    but i could not crack your clue
when you judge & juryed my statements
    believing them not true

by then i was bored with board-games
    so i thought to play my cards
i showed my hand you had me banned
    when i flashed my jack-of-hearts

by now i'd given up the game
    i knew i could not win
cos no matter how i played it
    you just would not let me in

*an insect fell onto a blade of grass*
*causing it to bend*
*from the path of the charging buffalo*

i was born in anguish
   could not believe the pain
i grew up but managed
   to come out right as rain


there were more tears than
             laughter
   in our broken home
arguing & fighting nurtured
   my sense to be alone


i have no wife or children
   i havent even friends
i'm under no illusions
   because i dont pretend


i spend my life by myself
   a life i do prefer
that way my life is not incensed
   by a family to which i won't
          concur


you may say i'm lonely
   but i know it isnt so
my little room is homely
   do as i please i just come & go

i have no one to bother with
    and no one bothers me
left to myself is all i wish
    thats how i like to be


### *plagiarised*

    walking into water without causing
a ripple
    entering a meadow without affecting
      a blade of grass
    a man of The Way transcends both
          cause & effect


    we were both the same age
      there for awhile
   when the baby smiled & waved
         at me
     for the first time

pulled out from my mothers womb
into a white tiled room
turned upside down & smacked
from that moment i wanted back
      between a womans thighs


placed upon my mothers teat
where i took my first feast
plucked away & put to bed
tasted tears the second shed
      a breast a place to lie


grew up round my mothers skirts
sanctuary i was not scared
then put to school amongst the boys
taken from my home & toys
      with no girls in sight


knocked around with all the lads
felt somehow that i'd been had
something missing i did not know
then it hit me like a blow
      i knew the reason why

then out into the world of men
in their bars & in their dens
excluded from the female form
a place i know was safe & warm
　　　"please help me back" i cry


*am trying to get some money*
*off the ground*
　　*to launch 'report'*
*then maybe sally forth*
　　*from plymouth*


if the rain rains
and the snow snows
why does the sun shine
instead of suns?

i can't take no more
i've paid my dues
i sed i can't take no more
i've paid my dues
am gonna close the last door
cos its time to leave this life blues

life is such a bore
so i'll say "adieu"
i sed life is such a bore
so i'll say "adieu"
i doe wanna take no more
cos it's time to leave this life blues

i've had my fill
its all bad news
i sed i've had my fill
its all bad news
i'm in for the kill (of me)
cos its time to leave this life blues

its time to ring the till
the payments overdue
i sed its time to ring the till
the payments overdue
have o.d.'d on lifes bitter pill
cos its time to leave this life blues

dont heed this advice
i'm no guru
i sed dont heed this advice
i'm no guru
we each have a choice (i've made mine)
cos its time to leave this life blues

to end ones life
is just taboo
i sed to end ones life
is just taboo
am sick & tired of strife
but not for you to leave this life blues

### *by brian with help*


My choices are made
Though there may be mistakes
My destiny makes its path from them

Shall I stay
Shall I go?
Choice changes the flow

Is it yes
Is it no
Shall I take them?

Or shall I decide
And cast choices aside
To let destiny make a path for me?

death stakes its claim in tears of
                    blood
the shamans dead but resurrects
his hood of white was clutched by K's
in a later age that burned with rage

sacred was the ground they sought
a people bought but were not sold
the gold was tarnished by their
                              greed
and a race that came to nought

put on a head-dress robes divine
dance primeval to unblinking sun
storm clouds gathered then came the
                                rain
but tourists laughed in scorn

a plague of Angles raped all lands
death in mind then on hands
death surrounds their very lives
shall they exterminate themselves?

from innocence to experience
i fell in one foul swoop
your lips told me their story
my heart tightened as in a hoop

your fingers traced the patterns
of a prison i could not break
and perfume clouded instincts
of bonds i could not shake

you caught me in your dreadful
                              web
deceit was overlaid
entanglement grew tighter
no matter how i prayed

lies became your trademark
as you drew me in
my tears lubricated laughter
as you mounted me on a pin

then stuck me in your album
a collection of broken hearts
put me in the show-case
of your lovers from the start

cannot take this worlds woes no more
am dying by degrees
cannot fight the foes no more
i'll just let it be

my death is not the answer
to basic questions not even asked
but tired of all the sorrow
so will take my life to task

i look beyond horizons
at those who wait at gates
and close my eyes to problems
for this will seal my fate

the spectre of starvation
stalks behind the walls
lift my voice to heaven
but no one hears my call

the storm clouds they are gathering
i hope there is still time
the hoards i pray are rising
have reached the end of line

death surrounds me i was the one
ghouls in glens & little girls
photographer had caught the face
screams pealed blackened by a trace

metal ripped agenst gods ghost
pass the wafer to the host
yellow flags they mark the path
to all who step before

black dress addresses uniform
gives her number "give me a call"
plane takes off then lands in crash
were all those deaths his fault?

red socks green socks take a step
"london" called on pavements cracked
banshees scream await the coach
the pilot waits his turn

wreckage deals his death his due
white hat & coat the morgue attends
necromancy murmurs shades of truth
as jackals take to fields

running lost through galleries waiting
                                to be found
surrounded by art thats run aground
    that grace the floor & walls
stake my claim amongst it all

critics feed crap crowds want pap
            New Age shines forth in '88
will clear the cobwebs this fresh broom
        sweeps
                        a breath of air from windows wide
                so obsolete & stale are brushed aside

a beacon proud for all to see
a clarion call over land & sea
            the four winds carry my message bright
                    sight & sound will flood about
                        to smash all barriers down

hear this voice dare this vision
unite divisions no matter creed
then greed & hunger we'll eradicate
        just step with me inside this gate

                        *dedicated to ben*

daring to think for myself i let loose
     my thoughts
     on an unsuspecting audience
daring to act for myself my actions
     awaken instincts long forgotten
         inside that audience
   think for yourself
   act for yourself

listen to me for just some moments
     come with me to that world within
where the concealed will be revealed

do not read & put aside but ponder
     ponder on my words profound
told before by many but now anew
digest this information told by
        an idiot i know
    though still an idiot full of
        sound & fury
     not the village but the worlds

     yes i do yes i dare
yes i'll share that world not out but in
     because without is from within
without is effect within the cause
   you cannot change without but within
and then youll live by laws eternal

which govern health wealth wisdom &
power
power to give as you start to receive
                            wisdom
            to do what is proper & right
                    wealth
            in abundance of what you want
                    and health
            to live your life to its most

                            *dedicated to angus*


*hiss of fire & rain*
*cry of gull & train*
*alone & lonely again*


i love to see washing billowing on the
line on a sunny windy day, especially
tee-shirts puffed out, almost as though
invisible muscular torsos were posing in
them

the waters cold but take the plunge
lunge into life, strength grows with
> strife
>> insides the power to overcome
>>> what may, you are the one


out theres the brink, do not think
> but act
the fact is, friends are there ready
>> to receive
> the you beneath veneer
that will unfold as the real comes
>> out


a seed is sown, shoots start growing
> when nurtured with adventure
the saplings strong, roots deep from
>> background
winds of adversity will bend but cannot
>>> break


the horizon awaits, do not hesitate
> that way leads to loss
you are the boss of all you survey
> if the way in your heart is love


*dedicated to john*

'slacker' by name but i hope not by
    nature
the failures within go out there and
    win
you have it inside do not hide your
      light
under a bushel or peck but what the heck
     go for it

you have the upbringing to bring forth
    the ammo
aim high for the stars & at least hit
    the moon
 its higher than earth
  you have the worth to make it

  dont waste all those talents
those talents inborn from the moment
    of birth
   generations past dont be the last
   but the first in line

you are the time you are the now
 and the here hear with the eyes
see with the ears then you will know
 that the way is clear for you to
    come through

*dedicated to slacker*

evil has made a home in my heart
hate congealed right from the start
when you left me for another
and that another was my brother
tore away a life from a wife & family
tore out the roots from a family tree


*dragonfly flits over pond*
*left of themselves*
*silent rings do not disturb...*


en-route to another nightmare
afraid of not knowing what the night
might bring
to go again through that hell
if only i knew what they foretell
it would be easier to face

bubbling from depths
inspiration wells up
breaking the surface
it floats to infinity
from whence it came


                                        prisoner of my dreams
                                            trying to escape
                                        shackled by fantasies
                                            i'll never make




the fruit from this tree
is ready for picking
please partake to dine & wine

distilled is stronger yet
but be careful of its strength
it can be heady

riding the wings of the morning wind
would that i could be by your side
just while the dew dries on the grass
to sit & pass a wine or two between
                                        ourselves

to talk about times long gone
when hand in hand we strayed along the
                        water-ways
and fed the golden carp in early morning
                        light
innocently speaking before this parting
that brought tears to both our eyes

the uncarved block is broken
myriad vessels strewn abroad
and i sent to this land of rain
to train these barbarous hordes to fish
                                and farm

i sit & dream of snow & sun
here each season mingles into one
all drab the difference being shades of
                                grey
with wetness in between

to be back in Three Rivers Kingdom
          half way to heaven
instead of here in the nether world
where women with painted faces ply their
         trade

to look upon your fair face once again
to kiss those natural lips
and touch that unadorned form
and be one with you once more

entwined upon our brocade couch
revelling away the night till dawn
to drink deep of your body
and you of mine
and together live out our time

                          ***apols li ling***

          the circle is unbroken
          before & aft the same
but the great whole must move forward
          nations shall know my name

i hire & fire who i like
hire & fire when i like
cos i'm a bastard

i'm in my prime
in this economic clime
pick & choose & youre bound to lose
cos i'm a bastard

i have all the Schemes to choose from
lawful slave labour at its best
i'm all for Victorian values
when i can feather my nest
cos i'm a bastard

my heroine is Thatcher
cos she's one of The Lads
us Lads all stick together
and you know that youve been had
cos we're all bastards

*re. illustrations*
*to some of my lyrics*
*i can visualise*
*but cannot materialise*

**before i'm dead my fame shall spread**
**this river will burst its banks**
**alluvial soil settles for seeds planted**
**in its wake**
**break through to sunlight my birthright**
**blossoms**
**pluck which blooms the mind entice**
**but root out only when you must**

Published in 1990
by
MANNAMEAD PRESS
77a, Mannamead Road
Mannamead
Plymouth PL3 4SX

7/8/90

Cover illustration © R.O.Lenkiewicz

ISBN 1 872606 00 8


Printed in England
by
North Print Press, Saltash
Typeset by Mannamead Press

produced

by

terrence neal haley

&

geoff holland

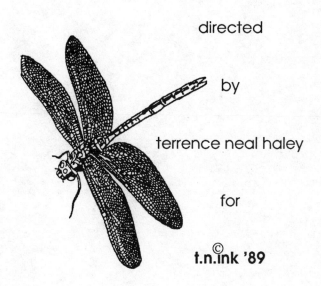

directed

by

terrence neal haley

for

t.n.ink '89